DOGS

WHO CHANGED THE WORLD

For Gary, my Border
terrier

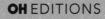

DOGS

WHO CHANGED
THE WORLD

DAN JONES

50 dogs who altered history,
inspired literature... or ruined everything

INTRODUCTION

Dogs are magic. Friend to the lonely, guide to the lost, muse to the artist and inappropriate poop-machines for the socially anxious. They have inspired great works of art, music and literature and travelled impossible distances to be reunited with their guardians. Others have caught spies, thwarted heists and reconnected lost lovers, dragged the drowning to safety or have just haplessly and happily ruined everything.

Dogs have trotted at our collective side for tens of thousands of years, bound up in the story of humanity. Starting with our first tentative relationship with the grey wolf through centuries of clever crossbreeding, domestication has seen the humble dog evolve from wild beginnings. They are tamer and calmer than their ancient ancestors, with the added superpower of being able to read human faces, understand language, and locate and chew your slippers beyond all recognition. And, with their senses forever turned up to 11, they constantly struggle to control their impulses and will therefore do almost anything for a slobbery tennis ball, a stick or a weird, dried cowpat to chew on.

These 50 tales are a celebration of our unbreakable relationship with the dog, the first ever domesticated animal, and their dogged dedication, heroism and unending sense of fun. Along the way we'll meet big-boned Barry, the hefty St Bernard credited with saving the lives of more than 40 lost souls in the Swiss Alps in the 1800s. We'll discover Sigmund Freud's calm-inducing chow chow, Jofi, who would sit in on his psychotherapy sessions (and never spilled a secret), and fall in love with Japan's tragic national hero Hachiko, famous for waiting for his dear-departed owner at Shibuya Central Station, becoming a much-loved local and national celebrity.

Dolly Parton wrote a heart-breaking ode to her childhood dog, Crackerjack, and Sir Isaac Newton's little terror Diamond played his own role in history, apparently knocking over a candle and destroying the physicist's most important manuscripts. Congratulate iconic actor and director Tilda Swinton's three beloved springer spaniels, who won the Palm Dog at the Cannes Film festival, and learn the true story of Laika, the intergalactic space dog.

Although most dog stories have love and longing at their heart, we haven't always treated our hairy friends with respect, and some heroic acts have come at quite a cost. Many have played a pivotal role in history (whether they wanted to or not), inspired passionate animal rights movements and helped us understand and reconsider our own very best qualities.

Dogs will frustrate you, confound you and leave you mystery gifts in the most unexpected of places, but if these stories prove anything, it is that dogs can enrich our world. They can transform the day-to-day experience of those with sense-loss or the neurodiverse, offering protection, comfort and guidance. They offer endless love and company for those who most need it. They'll go to the ends of the earth for you and completely transform your life if you let them. Like I said, dogs are magic. Let's meet some of these awe-inspiring canines.

HACHI

THE WORLD'S MOST LOYAL DOG

JAPANESE AKITA

First, there's the slow, sad *bing-bong* of the Shibuya train station ticket gates, then a rush of noise: overlapping digitised voices of ticket dispensers, commuter and tourist chatter, the chug of traffic. Cross over to the far edge of a square dotted with trees and people, lit by video screens, and there you'll find him, in front of Shibuya Scramble Crossing: the most famous and beloved dog in Japan.

On a simple stone plinth is the bronze statue of a dog called Hachiko, a pure-bred akita. The area, now known as Hachiko Square, is the busiest and best-known meeting spot in the heart of Tokyo and there is usually a small crowd around him, taking selfies, and holding their kids up to touch his paw, which is now worn smooth (he's been here

since 1948, recast from the original erected in 1934).

A bone's throw from the exit gate, it's the perfect spot for Hachiko, whose story of love, loyalty, and loss has enthralled Japan for decades. Trigger warning: it's a heartbreaker.

Hachiko wasn't always a city dog, and he wasn't always called Hachiko. He was born in the home of Mr Giichi Saito in Oshinai, Odate City, during the particularly chilly December in 1923. Hachiko's mother, Goma (which means 'sesame'), lived with her owner, Saito, in Akita Prefecture, and Hachiko's father was a handsome akita known as Oshinai.

Dr Hidesaburo Ueno was a scientist based at the Tokyo Imperial University. He loved the large, rambunctious, and princely *akita-inu* ('akita dog') but couldn't find the perfect example of the breed. One of his students told him about a litter in Odate and, on seeing them, Ueno was smitten. The newly born pup was sold for ¥30 (a rather large sum at the time) and, having waited until Hachiko was old enough, the scientist and his new chunky puppy returned to Tokyo by train the following January. During the 20-hour journey, something wonderful happened: they fell in love. Ueno named the pup Hachi, Japanese for number eight, which is considered lucky in Japanese (the '-ko' was added later).

Much like Hachi himself, the bond between the two grew fast and strong. They spent all their time together – Hachi would even insist on following Ueno to Shibuya train station every morning for Ueno's commute and would wait there all day to be reunited when his beloved owner returned each evening.

Akita are a highly intelligent, friendly, musclebound and big-boned breed, known for being extremely vigilant. They thrive on human companionship and are hard-wired to protect those they love.

When Hachi was six months old, everything changed. Dr Ueno waved goodbye to Hachi (who had, as always, insisted on following him), got on his morning train, and headed off to work. Only this time, Ueno didn't come home. Sadly, he suffered a brain haemorrhage at the university and died suddenly.

Hachi and Ueno had only been together for five months.

Hachi waited and waited but Ueno never returned. After the funeral, friends of Ueno moved Hachi to a new home a few kilometres away, but he would run away, only to be found inexplicably back at Shibuya station. Eventually, another friend, Ueno's onetime gardener Kikuzaburo Kobayashi, took Hachi in. He lived closer to Shibuya station and knew this might soothe Hachi's woes. After dinner each night, Hachi would return to

Ueno's old house and, never finding him there, would walk over to Shibuya station desperate to catch a glimpse of Ueno returning. Nothing could stop him. In fact, Hachi waited patiently for Ueno every single day – ignoring the heat, rain, snow and ice – for almost ten years.

At first, Shibuya commuters were perplexed. Just who was this gigantic, bear-like dog? And why was he sat every single day outside the ticket gates? Others were annoyed. They tried to chase him off and there are stories of Hachi being mistreated. But still, Ueno didn't come home.

Over the years, the story of Hachi began to spread. Staff at the station would look out for him, commuters might occasionally feed him, and in 1932, Hirokichi Saito of the Nihon Ken Hokonzai (The Association for the Preservation of the Japanese Dog) heard about him. He wrote about Hachi in the *Asahi Shimbun* newspaper and the story went viral. Readers fell in love with the star-crossed Akita, and he fast became a national icon. He became known as Hachiko, the 'ko' added to acknowledge his devotion and loyalty.

In fact, Hachiko made a star appearance at the unveiling of his own statue in 1934, enjoying the devotion and fame celebrity brings in the form of countless treats and fur-ruffles. But all he wanted was to see Ueno again.

After almost a decade of waiting for Ueno, Hachi finally passed away in 1934. He is remembered in statues and monuments – the most recent erected in 2015 on the nearby university campus – books, a museum, and big-budget movies. He was buried near Dr Ueno in the parkland of nearby Aoyama Cemetery, together again at last.

If you ever find yourself waiting for a loved-one in the noise and light of Shibuya station, be sure to pay your respects to the most loyal dog in the world.

MR FAMOUS

AUDREY HEPBURN'S SUPERSTAR DOG

YORKSHIRE
TERRIER

Meet mild-mannered Yorkshire terrier Mr Famous, the beloved dog of Audrey Hepburn, and the toast of Hollywood. Hepburn's love of Mr Famous knew few bounds. She went everywhere with him, from magazine cover shoots to celebrity parties, and he became her steadfast companion on set, riding in her bike basket as she pedalled around the film lot between takes. He even starred alongside Hepburn in *Funny Face* (1957) in the scene now referred to as the 'Anna Karenina' train shot, becoming as much part of her iconic look as her *Funny Face* wardrobe, which was designed exclusively by Hubert de Givenchy. The film, and Hepburn herself, were hugely influential in setting the style of the late 1950s and early 1960s, with Hollywood stars and Hepburn fans clamouring to dress like her. It is thought that

Yorkies became a firm fixture in the celeb community for this reason.

The Yorkshire terrier is one of the smallest, and arguably cutest, dog breeds, with long fine fur. Developed in Yorkshire, UK, in the nineteenth century, they are upbeat, playful dogs who suffer from separation anxiety. Although they seem happiest when in the arms of their owners, being taught to be independent without too much coddling can create a relaxed and confident dog.

Mr Famous wasn't the only canine love in Hepburn's life. She had a coterie of Jack Russells (Missy, Tuppy, Penny, Piceri and Jackie), a boxer, and she was an unabashed poodle lover, appearing in *Sabrina* flanked by a pair of extremely regal poodles. It was her beloved Mr Famous, though, who was Hepburn's headliner.

PICKLES

THE HEIST-THWARTING COLLIE
WHO SAVED THE 1966 WORLD CUP

COLLIE

In the run-up to the 1966 World Cup, the glittering prize – the Jules Rimet trophy – found itself swiped from an exhibition in Central Hall Westminster in London. A ransom was soon delivered (with the cup's removable lining as proof), with thieves demanding £15,000 in unmarked bills. The incident made headline news around the world and, with the tournament date just weeks away, the Football Association were frantic. An undercover police officer attempted a switch with the thief (with scrap paper standing in for the cash), but it all went horribly wrong and, although the police believed they had caught the culprit, the trophy itself was still missing. And then something rather wonderful happened.

Pickles, a small black-and-white collie who had no idea of the integral role he was about to play in international relations, set out for his morning walk. Snuffling underneath a bush in West Norwood, London, he found a parcel wrapped up in newspaper and string. Inside it? The trophy. Pickles became a star, his name known all around the world, and he even leveraged a small but impressive film career off the back of his heroism. England went on to win its first (and only) World Cup title after a feverish match against West Germany, and the trophy – presented by HRH Queen Elizabeth II – was finally held aloft by team captain Bobby Moore, thanks, in part, to Pickles.

GUNTHER III

ALL HAIL THE DOG MULTI-MILLIONAIRE

GERMAN
SHEPHERD

A handsome German shepherd, an impossibly rich countess, a multi-million-pound fortune and a mysterious group known as The Burgundians: it's a tale that might have come from the golden typewriter of Dan Brown. The story of Karlotta Leibenstein, a German countess and multi-millionaire who passed away in 1992, is legendary in dog circles. The story, that Karlotta left her considerable fortune to her beloved German shepherd Gunther III, has inspired column inches for decades. With more than $50M in the bank, Gunther and his heirs apparently joined an upper echelon of super-rich dogs who find themselves bequeathed gazillions.

With a portfolio managed by a team of Italian investors known as The Burgundians, Gunther's series of shrewd investments saw his – and his heirs' – wealth increase to hundreds of millions of dollars. In fact, there are countless articles revealing how the German shepherd enjoyed limo drivers and owned villas around the world, including one reportedly once owned by Madonna, and even owned an Italian regional football team.

But, like all the best Dan Brown pot-boilers, there is a twist in the tale. In November 2021 the Associated Press took down their evergreen Gunther profile, revealing the story to be a hoax. In fact, another more obscure article revealed the same in 2005: there was no Karlotta and no mysterious investment group. And Gunther was just a normal, if not abnormally handsome German shepherd who may or may not have been hired for appearances, perhaps as a publicity stunt to sell a house or two.

How Gunther's story has survived, unchecked, for so many years is something of a mystery. While it's not unusual for dogs to be part of their owner's will, inheriting such a large sum is rare. But the idea that a person might do anything for their dog, even leaving them a fortune, is easy to believe.

BOB

THE AUSTRALIAN TRAIN-HOPPER
OF THE 1800S

COLLIE CROSS

Bob, a cute collie-mix, was born in the early 1880s in South Australia. He was a teenage runaway who became enamoured with a group of nearby tracklayers and, at just nine months old, disappeared from his home. Picked up as a stray and employed as a guard dog, Bob was adopted by William Ferry, the assistant station master at Petersburg station (now known as Peterborough), and eventually found his way onto a passing train.

Thus began Bob's life as a full-time hitchhiker, living on locomotives and nestling into coal spaces close to his favourite train drivers. Bob – endearingly friendly – soon became an object of fascination for the engineers, trainmen and regular passengers, and the young mongrel was soon something of a national celebrity.

Hitchhiking, particularly on trains, isn't easy and Bob survived several accidents, until he could successfully jump from one moving train to another. He travelled thousands of miles across Australia, would bark at unruly passengers to keep them in line and, in 1895, Bob's fame went international via an article in UK periodical *The Spectator*. He died in 1897, known as the king of the outcasts, and is memorialised with a statue at Peterborough, which is still standing to this day.

STANLEY & BOODGIE

DAVID HOCKNEY'S ANTIDOTE TO GRIEF

DACHSHUND

Much is made of the love a dog can bring into a human's life, and many artists, writers and creatives have drawn on this unbreakable bond for inspiration. Not least David Hockney, the bespectacled British painter known for his decades-long career of wonky landscapes, gorgeously pastel-toned LA swimming pools, and his creative celebration of Stanley and Boodgie, Hockney's beloved dachshunds.

In 1995 David Hockney staged a UK exhibition entitled 'Dog Days', hanging 45 paintings of his two little sausage dogs to the walls of Salts Mill in his native Yorkshire. Stanley and Boodgie were Hockney's treasured companions and the exhibition – created in a feverish three months using easels set up around Hockney's house – is a love-letter to the dogs' sleeping, snuffling and farting.

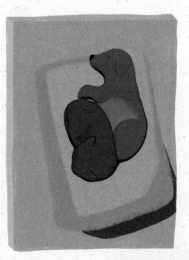

For reasons known only to themselves, artists love dachshunds. Warhol had Archie (he took him everywhere) and Picasso had Lump. Hockney was never far from Stanley and Boodgie, who lived with him in LA and frequented the dog parks of the Hollywood Hills. In the mid 1990s, at the height of the AIDS epidemic, Hockney tragically lost two thirds of his American friends to the disease, including four of his closest crew. And the artist had his own health challenges: his hearing had started to deteriorate in the early 1980s, cutting him off from music (another of his passions). His artistic focus on Stanley and Boodgie could be dismissed as mere idiosyncrasy, but Hockney had discovered something truly powerful: dog love soothes grief.

LAIKA

THE SPACE DOG

HUSKY-SPITZ CROSS

Laika is *the* intergalactic space dog – the first living creature (as far as we know) to orbit the Earth and the heroic comrade who helped the Soviet Union blast far, far ahead in the space race. She took off on 3 November 1957, neatly coinciding with the 40th anniversary of the Bolshevik Revolution on 7 November, and soared around the Earth.

In the 1950s and 1960s, the space race – an ideological and political competition between the US and the Soviet Union – had taken both countries by storm. Premier Nikita Khrushchev instructed Soviet engineers, fresh from the successful launch of the unmanned *Sputnik 1* vessel, to get their next project in the air ahead of their rivals – and it had to include a pressurised cabin and be scheduled close to the union's most auspicious date in just 32 days. The engineers raced to complete the project in time and, having achieved the almost impossible, were able to launch *Sputnik 2* on schedule with Laika, a stray husky-spitz cross, safely on board.

Months earlier Soviet canine recruiters had been tasked with rounding up a group of female strays from the Moscow streets. Moscow has long had its community of free-ranging dogs. They have appeared in Russian literature since the nineteenth century: Anton Chekhov wrote about them and Mikhail Bulgakov, *The Master and Margarita* author, celebrated them in his novella *Heart of the Dog*. They have adapted well to modern life and are often found on the metro system or waiting at pedestrian crossings, and they are skilled at begging for food. They became a problem in the 1990s with rather a few too many dangerous interactions with their human neighbours, but in

contemporary times they are usually caught, neutered and cared for.

The space dogs of 1957 were put through a type of astronaut training. They were tested in pressurised environments with loud noises, and one incredibly placid and friendly dog shone out. Kudryavka (Little Curly) was introduced to the Soviet nation on radio and barked out her greeting, earning herself a new name: Laika ('barker'). Just before the flight, Vladimir Yazdovsky, one of the dog specialists, took Laika home so she could enjoy some creature comforts before her intergalactic flight, and then, on 3 November, she took off from Tyuratam launch base in the Kazakh Republic and made history.

Some would like the story to end there, and for Laika, it did. She was sent into space with no hope of re-entry and no hope of survival, and for all the good work engaging the public with Laika and her part in the space race, there was a sense of regret in the swell of national pride. Although clearly ground-breaking, the intergalactic feat also highlighted the dubious ethics of using dogs and other animals in scientific and medical experiments. For Laika and the other dogs press-ganged into the programme, training had been arduous, involving days or weeks in pressurised cabins, and Laika and her back-up, Mushka, were operated on to embed medical monitoring equipment.

The capsule itself was cramped and hot, she was no doubt hungry (to conserve weight, only one meal was added to the payload) and she was forced into a spacesuit. The US was watching: the American National Air and Space Museum, reporting via the Smithsonian in 2018, noted that Laika's heartbeat was triple the normal rate (the museum owns declassified printouts from the time) and her breath was incredibly fast – she was terrified. Although she reached the peace of orbit alive, the heat shield had been lost and the temperature inside the capsule began to rise. Sputnik teams thought Laika would die painlessly of oxygen deprivation within seven days, but the tiny dog, alone in the emptiness of space, circled the Earth for just 102 minutes before she succumbed to the heat. One of Laika's trainers, Russian scientist and military man Oleg Gazenko, revealed in 1993 that Laika had died 'soon after launch'.

Laika was the first but not the last dog in space, and the Russians had already sent several canines on sub-orbital flights. The next dog-flight into orbit, *Sputnik 5* in 1960, was quite different, and there was every effort to bring tiny terriers Belka (Squirrel) and Strelka (Little Arrow) back to Earth. Along with a coterie of mice, rats and flies, they spent a day in space before returning to Earth alive. In fact, Belka and Strelka were the first ever living creatures to fly from Earth to the stars and make it all the way home again.

MAURICE

ANDY WARHOL'S POP ART IDOL

Bewigged American artist Andy Warhol was king of the Pop art movement, a shy, pale-as-a-ghost provocateur who lorded over the legendary musicians, models, celebs, drag queens, it-girls and oddballs of New York from the 1960s to the 1980s. Warhol was known for his many proclivities and peccadillos, but none so much as his love of dogs – dachshunds, to be precise. His beloved Archie truly earned his place in modern art's dachshund hall of fame: Warhol took him everywhere, even to famed club Studio 54, and was known to defer to him during celeb interviews if the journalist's questions bored him. But it was Maurice, Archie's transatlantic rival, who really caught Warhol's eye.

The artist – rarely known to turn down a commission – was invited to create a pet portrait of his friend Gabrielle Keiller's dachshund Maurice at the art collector's home in London. Working from Polaroids, Warhol created his masterpiece – and his screen-printed *Portrait of Maurice* in indigo, russet and pink hues is a stunner. Keiller donated her collection to the Scottish National Gallery of Modern Art in 1995 and Maurice's portrait was rediscovered – the museum's first ever Warhol artwork. No one knows how Archie truly felt about Maurice usurping his fame, but he may have made Warhol a little artwork of his own.

DACHSHUND

TEKA

THE AUSTRALIAN LIFESAVER

AUSTRALIAN
CATTLE DOG

The unstoppable Australian cattle dog, which counts the dingo as an ancestor, is known for its ingenuity, independent nature, rippling muscles and dogged dedication to its owner. Teka, a female Aussie cattle dog, took that dedication to another level.

In 2007 Teka's owner, Jim Touzeau, a glass craftsman, took her to work. But the 79-year-old suffered a heart attack and collapsed unconscious on the factory floor. Teka – an extremely watchful and alert dog – knew immediately that something was wrong. She climbed onto his chest and, with her significant weight, began to jump repeatedly. She also barked loudly in Jim's face before running outside to raise the alarm. Her jumping and barking revived Jim enough for him to call out for help and, miraculously, he was saved.

'I don't know if she actually kick-started my heart,' said Jim in an interview with his local newspaper, the *Brisbane Times*, 'but the doctors said that if I hadn't come to and called for help the chances are I would be dead.' Although medics were unable to say whether Teka's CPR had any physiological impact, Jim knew better – he's confident that he would not be alive if it wasn't for his beloved cattle dog.

Six years before the incident, Jim lost his wife. 'It's a pretty lonely life on your own,' he said. But three years later, Teka came into his life. 'She's a terrific companion,' Jim said. 'She just never leaves my side. Because it's just the two of us, I rely on her, and she relies on me.'

SEÑOR XOLOTL

FRIDA KAHLO'S TRUE MUSE

XOLOITZCUINTLI

In *The Love Embrace of the Universe, the Earth, Myself, Diego and Señor Xolotl* (1949), iconic artist Frida Kahlo paints a truly trippy self-portrait. She is held in a loving embrace at the centre of the universe with everything she adores close to her. In her arms, a baby-like version of her husband, Diego Rivera (with a flaming crotch), and nearby? Her dog, Señor Xolotl. It's a dog lover's fever dream.

Kahlo's near-hairless, whippet-like xoloitzcuintli is a rare and ancient breed, once prized by the Aztecs and a mainstay of Mesoamerican art. The Aztecs and Mayans thought of the 'xolo' as healers (they make excellent snuggle buddies, warming the extremities of those who are gravely ill), and they revered this skinny, super-intelligent dog, an ancestor of the Mexican hairless Chihuahua. Kahlo felt the same, and Señor Xolotl – named after an Aztec deity and guardian of the underworld – appeared in many of the artist's self-portraits, alongside her wild menagerie of animals (Kahlo's beloved pets appear in about a third of her works).

Despite its rich history and near-regal status, the xolo only achieved American Kennel Club official recognition in 2011, perhaps because its looks have always split opinion. With our contemporary obsession towards hyper-cute dogs with pristine, luxurious fur and teddy bear eyes, this ancient breed has always confounded. But for Kahlo, beauty was a hairless xolo.

BODHI

MEET THIS CHARMING MAN, THE MENSWEAR DOG

SHIBA
INU

For starters, Bodhi is handsome, even for a shiba inu. He's all big shoulders and sparkling eyes, has a great set of bright white gnashers and an expertly groomed tail. He looks as good dressed down in a simple hoodie and car coat as he does in a tux, accessorised with a few vintage gold chains. It's no wonder he's a menswear icon.

In 2013 Bodhi's owners, New York fashion designer Yena Kim and her graphic designer partner David Fung, had a thought that has crossed the mind of almost all dog owners at one time or another: would my dog look cute in a leather biker jacket and beanie? They brilliantly styled Bodhi up in a few menswear outfits and tentatively uploaded the images to Instagram as @mensweardog. Little did they know they had begun the slow pivot to a new international celebrity brand. Bodhi's portraits gained a steady social media following and soon the brands came knocking. Fashion retailers

– wowed by Bodhi's innate sense of style and cult following – lined up to collaborate with him. From luxury houses like Coach, Brooks Brothers, and Salvatore Ferragamo to more affordable retailers like ASOS, Bodhi was in demand.

Under the stewardship of Yena and David, Bodhi is big business. He has modelling contracts, fashion collabs, a book, column inches in *The New York Times*, *GQ* and *TIME* magazine, and in 2018 he launched his own fashion collection for humans. Of course, it helps that Bodhi looks great in almost anything. He might wear a fedora on the sidewalks of Brooklyn, or style it up with a fresh gingham shirt, sprawled out on a picnic rug in the summer sun. His Wall Street suits have *American Psycho* vibes, and his suede Baker Boy and ribbed Brooks Brothers sweater look (as he silently salivates over a croissant at a street cafe) is pure Serge Gainsbourg.

TAIL

THE NON-MAGICAL MAGICAL DOG OF CHINESE LEGEND

UNKNOWN

Ancient Chinese stories are full of very good boys – divinely inspired, heroic dogs whose loyalty, strength and devotion are the stuff of legend. There's Panhu, the five-coloured dog who could transform into a human (if he stayed under a giant golden bell for seven days). He famously helped Emperor Ku win a battle, slaying invaders and bringing his owner the head of his enemy; he was married off to Ku's daughter for his troubles. Panhu is second only to Tiangou, or 'Heavenly Dog', who was extremely food-motivated and loved to eat celestial bodies; you can spot him in ancient Chinese art as a meteor or comet. So far, so fantastical, but the ancient stories are full of delightful non-magical dogs too.

A novel from the Northern Song Dynasty (960–1127), *The Saviour with a Tail*, is a perfect illustration of the Chinese love of dogs. In the story, Hualong's dog, nicknamed Tail, would accompany him on hunting trips. One day, on a local riverbank, Hualong was attacked by a python – saving his owner from certain death, Tail bit the snake to death. With Hualong unconscious, Tail raised the alarm by running back home to alert his family. They found Hualong, rushed him home and nursed him back to health, with Tail refusing to eat for two days until his owner woke up again. So even non-magical dogs can be magic sometimes.

SPICEDOGSSS

THE CUTE A.F. DOG PACK RIDING THE KOREAN WAVE

POODLE

In recent years the world has been delightfully and willingly gripped by South Korean pop culture, including music, TV and film, gaming, art, fashion and cuisine. This Korean Wave – aka *hallyu* (a Chinese term) – has thrown the spotlight on creative exports like the supremely talented boyband BTS, all-female supergroup Blackpink and gory Netflix mega-hit *Squid Game*.

Since 2000, or thereabouts, the phenomenon first hit China, then Japan and Southeast Asia before continuing its thrilling international tour, Gangnam Style. The wave has created a resurgence of contemporary South Korean creativity, satisfying feverish pop fans and high-brow critics alike, and giving an economic boost to the South Korean economy. No small part of that wave is the Spice Dogs, two pastel-macaron-coloured poodles (and their mini pup friends), beloved by adoring fans across the world. Meet Gappy and Mayo and their friends Kkanppi, Yeppi, Hodu, Hoochu, Saeng-Gang, Manool, Bulggul and Mugmul, all *hallyu* Instagram superstars. Like their K-Pop counterparts, the Spicedogsss have their own popular product line, but most follow the dogs for their fashion looks. Favourite outfits include bejewelled pastel harnesses, summer skirting in broderie anglaise (perfect for a picnic), Victorian pool outfits with ruffled swim caps, and their collab with dog outfitters Babirin, which takes the form of a walk-in wardrobe with hundreds of dog looks.

BUMMER & LAZARUS

MEET THE PROFESSIONAL SCALLYWAGS

MONGREL &
NEWFOUNDLAND

Before its recent tech-bro and vegan bubble tea incarnation, San Francisco had long been a Nirvana for waifs and wastrels, hippies and oddballs, and alternative counterculture types. In the 1860s professional chancers Bummer (a stocky black-and-white Newfoundland) and Lazarus (a yellow-black mongrel) were no different. This pair of canine street urchins trotted down the city's Montgomery Avenue and into local legend. The two dogs, both homeless, were as thick as thieves and worked as an inseparable duo to steal food, earn treats and – somewhat unfathomably – solve mysteries. With a reputation in the local press, lampooned in cartoons, and exempt from the dogcatcher, it wasn't Bummer and Lazarus' relationship to humans that endeared them to San Franciscan society, but their dogged devotion to each other.

At first, Bummer was a solo artist on Montgomery Street,

helpfully catching the odd rat outside a saloon popular with journalists. Then Bummer stepped in and saved another dog who'd been fighting a much larger opponent, but his new friend was gravely wounded. Bummer stayed close and – miraculously – the smaller dog recovered. The local newspapermen named him Lazarus, and from then on they were bonded for life. The pair earned themselves a reputation as talented rat catchers (their record was 85 kills in 25 minutes) and even discovered the whereabouts of a runaway horse.

Whether it was the feverish fame-building of the journalists or Bummer and Lazarus' natural charm, the pair left an unforgettable imprint in San Franciscan history. They are immortalised with a plaque in the Redwood Grove public space and in these poetic words first printed in the *San Francisco Bulletin*: 'Two dogs with but a single bark, two tails that wagged as one.'

FILOU

KING LOUIS XIV'S FROU-FROU LITTLE POODLE

POODLE

To Paris, the mid-to-late 1600s, and the court of the bewigged Sun King himself, Louis the Great, or just plain old Louis XIV. His magnificent, near-magical life of opulence and adventure made him the trendsetter of his day: his '*oui*' or '*non*' would set crazes, break hearts or flounder whole industries. The King of France ruled from Versailles – a shimmering, showy, illuminated palace that became the epicentre of French culture, and it remains so entrenched in the French identity that if you hear '*C'est pas Versailles ici!*' today you've no doubt left the light on. Along with writers like Molière and Racine, and countless painters, musicians and architects, there was another delightful artform Louis loved: his coterie of tiny poodles, led by national celebrity and star poodle Filou. Louis' love of poodles was shared by the entire French court, and the dogs themselves – descendants of German aquatic retrievers known as *pudels* – were given frou-frou haircuts, ranging from pompadours to moustaches, and were carried around like priceless artefacts.

Perhaps this poodle-as-fashion-accessory origin has led to the poodle being dismissed as a lamebrain, folly of a dog, but the breed is rather special. Intelligent, affectionate and athletic, with a low-allergen coat, the poodle is the perfect (and popular) crossbreed, and purebred poodles are often perfect for therapy dog roles. What was adored by Louis was adored by the cream of French society, and Filou and the poodle breed became synonymous with the great nation. But we can thank Louis for also associating the poodle with the idea of opulent celebrity, something just as resonant 300 years later. *Merci*, Louis and Filou!

SALTY & ROSELLE

THE GUIDING-EYE DOGS OF 9/11

LABRADOR

Salty could dart through a crowd, sensing gaps before they appeared, and shoot through, leading his owner Omar Rivera to safety. As a guide dog, Salty's first beat was Yorktown Heights in North Westchester, but part of his training included trips to New York City to ride the subway, skilfully ignoring hotdog stands and the traffic-choked avenues of the Bronx; he was well versed in navigating rush hour. 'He was definitely a city dog,' his trainer Caroline McCabe-Sandler said.

A pale-golden Labrador retriever (a breed known for its intelligence, playful attitude, and all-round waggy-tail friendliness), Salty graduated from Guiding Eyes for the Blind in Westchester County in 1998. Standards are extremely high for a guide dog and not every pup makes the grade. McCabe-Sandler, who also trains dogs to work with children on the autism spectrum, placed her star pupil with Omar Rivera, a Westchester man living with vision loss.

On September 11, 2001, Salty helped guide Rivera to work on the 71st floor of tower one of the World Trade Center (One WTC). They arrived early, at around 7am, and Rivera, who worked in IT, had a meeting to prepare for with the Port Authority of New York and New Jersey. At about 8:45am, Rivera was ready to go, with Salty dozing peacefully at his workstation. He heard the unplaceable sound he would later

understand to be American Airlines Flight 11, hijacked and crashing into the tower, 22 floors above him. The building shook, Rivera's computer fell to the floor, and Salty – clearly disturbed – ran up and down a hallway close to Rivera's desk. Something extraordinary had happened.

Salty wasn't the only guide dog working in One WTC that day. Just seven storeys up, on the 78th floor, worked sales director Michael Hingson, another man with vision loss, and his own guide dog, golden Labrador retriever Roselle. Roselle was a Californian girl, blonde as the day is long. Having been trained at Guide Dogs for the Blind in San Rafael, in 1999 she took the place of Hingson's fifth guide dog.

Hingson and Roselle had also started their day a little earlier than usual, just like Rivera and Salty, and had travelled in from New Jersey via taxi and the PATH train. Hingson had set up the conference room for a breakfast meeting and Roselle was waiting close to the door to greet the attendees. And then the plane hit. In the moments immediately afterwards, Roselle remained so incredibly calm that, for a moment, Hingson thought things might not be so serious after all. But then the reality of the situation hit. 'Tearfully, colleagues said goodbye to each other. I was sure I was going to die,' said Hingson in 2011. He started his evacuation down the stairwell, with Roselle guiding him and 30 of his co-workers. 'If she had sensed danger

she would have acted differently, but she didn't,' said Hingson. 'Roselle and I were a team and I trusted her.'

The stairwell – full of the scent of smoke, falling debris, and the cries of the hundreds of people – took a gruelling hour to descend. Omar Rivera held onto Salty's harness and started the long journey to the ground floor. Soon, the stairwell became too crowded, too confusing, and it was suggested Rivera let go of Salty's harness so both could move more easily. But abandoning his owner was quite simply against Salty's training. He refused to leave Rivera's side. Rivera's supervisor, Donna Enright, helped the pair descend further, and when another co-worker tried to help by taking hold of the harness, Salty again refused. He would not leave Rivera.

At the same moment, Roselle was guiding Michael Hingson through the same experience, keeping incredibly calm, staying close to his side. By the time Salty, Roselle, and their owners reached the street outside, Two WTC collapsed, engulfing them in dust and debris. Rivera and Salty were less than three blocks away; they had got out just in time. Roselle calmly led Hingson through the dust and confusion to a subway station, where they found and helped a woman who had been blinded by falling debris.

Salty and Roselle received a joint award for their incredible and no-doubt life-saving work. The

Dickin Medal from the People's Dispensary for Sick Animals in 2002 was inscribed with the following: 'For remaining loyally at the side of their blind owners, courageously leading them down more than 70 floors of the World Trade Center, and to a place of safety following the terrorist attack on New York on September 11, 2001.'

Salty passed away in 2008, and Roselle in 2011. 'Trust: that's the most important thing in a relationship with a guide dog,' said Rivera in the 2011 Nat Geo documentary *Where Were You*. Salty was Rivera's third guide dog, an essential companion for the man who had lost his sight when he was 28. 'They give everything they have for almost nothing, just for love.'

THE BASKERVILLE HOUND

THE ORIGIN STORY OF SHERLOCK'S GREATEST ADVERSARY

In Sir Arthur Conan Doyle's 1902 mystery novel *The Hound of the Baskervilles*, the author's famously idiosyncratic detective Sherlock Holmes is drawn into an almost supernatural mystery on the misty, lonely uplands of Dartmoor in southern England. In the story Sir Charles Baskerville has been found dead in the garden of his manor house and the family, it is said, has been cursed by a demonic hound. Professional sceptic Sherlock immediately scoffs at the idea of a curse, but as he embroils himself in the world of the moors, it seems things are not quite as they should be.

Much of the inspiration for *The Hound* came from Doyle's research into the Dartmoor and ancient English folklore that echoes throughout the book. Inspiration seems to be focused on the deliciously creepy story of Squire Richard Cabell of Buckfastleigh in Devon, who had apparently murdered his wife and sold his soul to the devil. When Cabell died in 1677, a pack of ghostly hounds were seen thundering across Dartmoor coughing up flames only to howl at his tomb (a phenomenon thought to happen to this day on the anniversary of Cabell's death). Spoiler alert: the hellish beast of *The Hound of the Baskervilles* turns out to be an ordinary if very angry dog, a patsy for a murderous plot to claim an inheritance, but Doyle's novel – and the legends he drew on – still resound to this day. The 'Baskerville Effect' is a somewhat unfashionable psychological term to describe the superstitious who have seemingly died in fright. The nightmarish story of an evil black dog haunts the legends of old England – with such creepy canines as the Yeth hound, the Barghest and Shuck the Dog-Fiend, who stalks the coastline at night – but surely there can be no truth in these tales? Like Sherlock says to Dr Watson, 'Presume nothing.'

NEVILLE JACOBS

THE HARDEST-WORKING DOG IN FASHION

Meet 'the hardest-working dog in fashion', according to New York's *T* magazine: a handsome bull terrier known as Neville Jacobs. Neville shares his Frank Lloyd Wright-designed abode in Rye, Westchester County, NY, with fashion designer Marc Jacobs and his husband, Char Defrancesco, and lives the life most dogs could only dream of.

Before moving upstate, for most of his life Neville was a busy downtown NYC dog, trotting to and from his Upper West Side townhouse and the Marc Jacobs atelier. His day-to-day schedule is documented on Instagram, showing walks around the city parks of New York City to fashion gatherings and rides in a luxury jet to locations all over the world (all of which gives Marc Jacobs fans, which are legion, a glimpse into the designer's own life in the process).

Like many native New Yorkers, bull breeds are tough but have a great sense of humour. They (bull breeds, not New Yorkers) are usually muscular, hardy and need lots of exercise, but are also playful and devoted, and are far gentler than the sometimes-bad reputation of the breed suggests. Neville has an adorable disposition, and his own sense of style is unparalleled, not just for a dog. He has become something of a cultural influencer and looks incredible in a Marc Jacobs chunky knit. Neville even has an authorised biography, *Neville Jacobs: I'm Marc's Dog,* by Nicolas Newbold, which was published by the prestigious Rizzoli in 2016. But does all this undeniable jet-set fame go to Neville's head? Of course not. Although he has held audience with fashion royalty like Christy Turlington and Karlie Kloss, and has visited the most glamorous locations on the planet, to Neville a lamp-post is a lamp-post, wherever in the world he is.

BULL
TERRIER

FIPS

EDVARD MUNCH'S INSPIRATION

FOX TERRIER

To Norway, and the iconic yet tortured art of Edvard Munch (1863–1944), whose psychological 'soul painting' approach saw him explore his psychic dread through expressionistic, dreamlike pastels and oils. His most famous work, *The Scream*, has been endlessly co-opted, reworked and meme'd, immortalised as fridge magnets, phone cases and even thongs, such is the enduring resonance of the artist's depiction of anguish. But even Norwegian despair-artists need to take a break.

Enter the humble dog, Munch's greatest inspiration. After time in Paris and Berlin, and periods of heavy drinking and anxiety (following the deaths of his mother and sister in 1908), the artist lived in almost self-sufficient solitude in Oslo, with only his dogs for company. His fox terrier Fips was closest to his heart; in a letter to writer Christian Gierløff, Munch wrote that 'an old wise man's soul has taken up residence' in his dog. Soon, Boy joined the pack, an affectionate Gordon setter, and then a lolloping St Bernard known as Bamse (Norwegian for 'teddy bear').

The artist and his dogs were inseparable; they were even known to accompany him to the local cinema, and if they barked, he would interpret it as a bad review and would leave before the credits rolled. And, although Munch adored almost all canines, he was less than enamoured with his neighbour's dog, Rolle, who once ripped the trousers off a postman (and who is thought to be the subject of *Angry Dog*). Munch both painted and drew his dogs, and Fips is thought to be the star of his lauded *Head of a Dog* painting, a work not saturated with despair but rather a tiny flash of hope.

BAEKGU

THE JINDO OF DONJI-RI, SOUTH KOREA

JINDO

Welcome to Jindo, the almost mythical (but very real) 'Dog Island', a South Korean isle just southwest of the Korean Peninsula, and home to the village of Donji-ri. It is here that the Jindo dog originates, South Korea's most celebrated breed and an official national treasure. Boy, are they cute – with their perked ears and shining eyes. They have many of the hallmarks of the Japanese shiba inu: hyper-real cuteness and a certain regal air.

The Jindo's temperament is legendary: they are watchful (and make great guard dogs), super intelligent and fiercely loyal. In fact, such is their loyalty, there are stories (or are they legends?) of Jindo dogs travelling hundreds of kilometres to be reunited with their owners, or holding vigil over the recently deceased, refusing

to eat. For hundreds of years, it is thought the Jindo dogs were near-wild on the island, living in harmony with residents, and there are many legends of the breed's almost-symbiotic relationship with the island community. Now, there's a small Jindo dog theme park, an island-wide national Jindo dog holiday, and a dog contest with many – if not most – breed families of Jindo. One of the most famous Jindo dogs was known as Baekgu (or 'a white dog') who, in 1993, is thought to have travelled 186 miles south from Daejeon to be reunited with her previous owner (a bridge connects Jindo to the mainland). Baekgu soon became a national obsession, with journalists flocking to Jindo, and Baekgu appearing in cartoons, kids' books and even an opera.

MARNIE

THE FIRST DOG INFLUENCER

SHIH TZU

There was a time when the late, great Marnie was the most famous living dog in the world. She had 1.7 million Instagram followers, had received hugs from Miley Cyrus, Tina Fey, Taylor Swift and Lena Dunham, and had trotted into the hearts of dog-lovers worldwide with her superior understanding of social media platforms (remember Vines?). The NYC-based shih tzu, known for her tilted head and impossibly long tongue, was the world's first dog influencer. Dogfluencer, if you will.

But every celebrity story starts somewhere, and in her previous life, Marnie was an abandoned dog eking out an existence on the streets of Connecticut. When she was finally picked up by animal control in 2012, she was in a sorry state, with matted fur, decaying teeth, and a clouded eye. She also lived with vestibular syndrome, a not-uncommon condition that can cause a dog's head to tilt. Known briefly as Stinky, she was thought to be around 10 years old. But when her future owner, Shirley Braha, met her after four months in an animal shelter, she saw something truly special in the delightfully wonky-looking

♥ | ○ ○ ○ ○ ○

shih tzu, and the pair hot-footed it to New York City. When Braha tentatively began posting Marnie content online, her cuteness shone through, and she soon became the poster girl for senior dog adoption.

More than 7.5 million animals enter shelters in the US each year. Of those, 3.9 million are dogs and approximately 1.2 million go on to be euthanised. Many senior dogs are overlooked for adoption, but those who take up the leash can find it a truly rewarding experience. Senior dogs can often be calmer, less destructive, and tend to need less exercise than their younger counterparts, and even the most maltreated and unlucky dogs, given the right kind of love and care, seem to thrive.

Marnie passed away in 2020, leaving behind a wealth of celeb pics, a book and even an app, but also a fund, Marnie's Old Pals, focused on access for senior dogs in shelters to veterinary care. She also raised a huge amount of awareness for the plight of dogs once considered a little too long in the tooth.

ROSY, DORA & SNOWBEAR

TILDA SWINTON'S AWARD-WINNING SPRINGER SPANIELS

SPRINGER
SPANIEL

'I have to tell you honestly, this is the prize to get,' proclaimed actor, director, cultural behemoth and chameleon of the silver screen Tilda Swinton on accepting the Palm Dog Award on behalf of her springer spaniels at the Cannes Film Festival in 2021.

Swinton's dogs were nominated, in part, for their performance with Swinton and her daughter Honor Swinton Byrne in *The Souvenir Part II*. But Rosy, Dora and Snowbear are also the stars of Swinton's self-made music video to one of Handel's operatic masterpieces, 'Rompo i lacci', from his opera *Flavio*, for Opera Philadelphia's Glass Handel project. The video shows Swinton's springer spaniels gallivanting around on a beach in slow motion – and then comically sped up – and quite plainly having the time of their young lives.

The award is not strictly affiliated with the official festival, but who cares about such trifles? We can thank British journo Toby Rose for basically making 'fetch' happen by keeping the odd little award in the press since 2001. Another notable honouree is Sayuri, who had a starring role as Brandy in Quentin Tarantino's *Once Upon a Time... in Hollywood*.

MOPS

THE IMAGINARY PUG OF MARIE ANTOINETTE

PUG

Brioche, big hair, the guillotine and pugs: the enduring celebrity of Marie Antoinette (1755–1793) is marked by the most important objects of her life. The tragic Queen of France may now largely be remembered for her misguided solution to national poverty (aka brioche), but her towering, gravity-defying wigs and her grisly end are second only (as far as this book is concerned) to her love of pugs. And one pug in particular: dear little Mops.

The legend of Mops, whose name pokes its pudgy head up throughout history, is thus: as a young archduchess in Austria, Marie Antoinette (born Maria Antonia) adored the company of Mops, her tawny little pug, but on moving to France to be married to Louis-Auguste at the age of 14, she was forced to leave Vienna without him (a dog seemed unbecoming for such

a lady). Marie Antoinette pined for Mops and, sure enough, he was finally sent to the French court for them to be reunited in a show of the young dauphine's growing influence. When Louis finally parked his *derrière* on the throne in 1774, Marie Antoinette became the last Queen of France, and other dogs were added to the household. In fact, a little spaniel, Thisbe, stayed with the queen and her children while Louis was beheaded. They were finally separated when the queen herself was led to the guillotine – Thisbe reappeared when the deed was done, letting out a pained howl.

Although there are many details about Marie Antoinette's life that stand up to scrutiny (being the owner of one of the world's first flushing toilets is one of them), unfortunately the legend of Mops does not. The little pug is thought not to have existed at all, but the

idea of him has echoed throughout the young queen's story, and most biographers write as though he was real. The queen did in fact request a 'mops' dog, referring to the breed we now know as the pug, and the story of her being separated and reunited with a particular dog started to take shape. But there's more to the story, especially from a contemporary viewpoint. Marie Antoinette was a child, alone at the French court, her life and body traded for political gain, and the court itself was full of jealousy and ill-will. Wouldn't a pug have been a huge comfort to a child facing the unimaginable? Let's bid *au revoir* to Mops, the little pug who lived in the imagination of Marie Antoinette ... and in our imagination too.

ZEUS

TRULY THE GREATEST GREAT DANE

In Greek mythology, Zeus was the god of sky and thunder – a lusty, bearded super-being who lorded over the other gods with his mighty wrath, supernatural abilities and unmatchable stature. Aeons later, Kevin and Denise Doorlag of Otsego, Michigan, were falling in love with their own little super-being, a gangly black great dane puppy. Denise wanted a 'big name' for their soon-to-be big dog, but Kevin wanted something cuter. In the end, they drew inspiration from the ancient times and Denise won out; they named their puppy Zeus. Denise was right to pick a big name. He grew and grew, eventually surpassing all recorded metrics for great danes. At full adulthood, on his hind legs, Zeus was an astonishing, record-breaking 2.23m (7ft 4in) tall.

Great danes are descended from sixteenth-century European hunting dogs (themselves a crossbreed of English mastiffs and Irish wolfhounds), who were used to hold down large prey, like bears and deer, which had been hunted by other, nimbler breeds. But by the late 1800s great danes were no longer working dogs and were considered a luxury, and today their hunting instinct is second only to being a lanky, affectionate and slightly farty presence in family homes. The breed is known for its gentle, laid-back personality and ability to easily build relationships with humans and pets.

Sadly, the greatest things are destined to burn bright but for half the time, and the life-expectancy for large dog breeds is generally much lower than for your average tiny terrier. Zeus passed away in 2014 at the tender age of five. A certified therapy dog who visited people at a nearby hospital, Zeus also achieved another near-godly accolade in his lifetime: the Guinness World Record for the 'world's tallest canine'. The greatest great dane now has his own mythology.

KABOSU

THE CRYPTOCURRENCY ICON

SHIBA INU

Say *hajimemashite* to Kabosu, the Japanese shiba inu who launched a thousand memes, broke a million hearts and is, somewhat confoundingly, the face of cryptocurrency Dogecoin. Kabosu is the drop-dead gorgeous female shiba inu whose unsuspecting owner featured a cute portrait of her dog on a blog in 2010. Soon, the photo – overlaid with rainbow-coloured Comic Sans text – started to appear online as a meme. Meme-world is a dark, unpredictable place – akin to the Marvel Studios multiverse, with its endless remixing of characters and ideas – and soon Kabosu's photo was everywhere. Online communities on 4chan and Reddit swamped the internet with new versions, and by 2013 the meme – and, unwittingly, Kabosu – began to enter the collective consciousness.

Kabosu is a calm and friendly rescue dog who, as a puppy, ended up in an animal shelter with 19 other pedigree shiba inu when a local puppy mill closed down. She was adopted in 2008 by kindergarten teacher Atsuko Satō, who started a blog to raise awareness of the dangers of puppy mills and to promote dog adoption (the blog, incidentally, is one of the most popular pet sites in Japan). While Kabosu's 'doge' meme was growing,

the pair were simply living their best lives, blissfully unaware of Kabosu's growing fame.

Just when it couldn't get any sillier, in 2013 software engineers Billy Markus and Jackson Palmer created a new cryptocurrency, intending it to be a joke to poke fun at the obsession with the crypto-finance world. And who better than to front the new product but Kabosu's doge meme? The Dogecoin was born, and instead of garnering a few upvotes on Reddit, the currency did rather well (and is now worth millions). Today, Kabosu's fame is international, but in the West, she is thought of first as a meme. In Japan, she and Atsuko Satō are true celebrities, just as it should be.

DAVID, BILLY & COLETTE

RADCLYFFE HALL & THE DOGS OF LESBIAN JOY

BULLDOG

Radclyffe Hall (1880–1943) is the pioneering lesbian author whose gender non-conforming and lusty lifestyle and electrifying, taboo-breaking novel *The Well of Loneliness* (1928) have inspired gay women for more than half a century. Hall lived life just as she liked – a radical act for a woman in the late 1800s and early 1900s – with her dachshunds and French bulldogs (and lovers) trotting obediently by her side.

Hall dressed in men's clothing (from perfectly tailored, bespoke suiting to a leather riding coat and a jaunty Spanish riding hat), called herself 'John' and (eventually) lived with her female partner Una Troubridge. Hall's fame as an outspoken, confident figure and her powerful stature is celebrated in paintings and photographs, and these often featured Hall and Troubridge's gaggle of dogs, including Billy and Colette – the pair adored attending legendary dog show Crufts.

With Hall and Troubridge living their best, dog-filled, lesbian lives, at the same time a young woman called Monica Still was trying to do the same. She met Marya Burrell in Hastings, close to Hall's house in nearby Rye. Both 19-year-old nurses, the young lovers were thrilled by Hall's fame and her almost-magical proximity, and they embarked on a secret affair. Born to wealth and privilege, Hall's

status allowed her to subvert societal norms and express her sexuality within a sort of social eccentricity, but others from more lowly backgrounds were not so lucky. In *The Well of Loneliness*, Stephen, the young female protagonist, falls in love with Mary, an older ambulance driver in WWI, only for the pair to suffer rejection from a cruel society; in the real world, Monica and Marya parted after a single year of love and soon lost touch.

Almost 30 years passed until the quiet power of dogs brought Monica and Marya back together. In the early 1970s Monica appeared in a television commercial for a brand of dog food. Gay and lesbian life in the UK had changed, and seeing her on screen, Marya knew she must reach out to her true love. They were reunited after three decades and soon visited the tomb of Radclyffe Hall in Highgate Cemetery, London. They were shocked to find it in a state of disrepair and set about to raise funds for its upkeep. The pair raised thousands of pounds to pay for its restoration, and in 1994 Monica, aged 71, was present at an informal ceremony to mark its success. They had spent the last seven years of Marya's life in Wittisham, Kent, not far from Rye, where they started the Radclyffe Hall Memorial Fund. Marya died in 1988 at the age of 63.

Dogs also played a fateful role in the lives of Hall and Troubridge.

The pair spent the night together in Maidenhead after buying a bulldog, and Troubridge, on returning to her partner Ladye Batten, was involved in a row that left Batten dead from a stroke. Hall and Troubridge (who had been having an affair) finally announced themselves as a couple and devoted much of their time to their dogs. They even visited a medium, who attempted to contact the soul of one of their departed pups, and they were happy to pose in all manner of society photographs with their favourite canines.

Hall hoped *The Well of Loneliness* might allow for a 'more tolerant understanding' of lesbians and gay men – who she described as 'some of the most persecuted and misunderstood people in the world'. Although it faced censorship and was banned for a time, the book certainly changed the lives of women like Monica and Marya. In the book itself, Stephen and Mary have their own dog, David. Hall wrote of David's waggy-tailed love of Stephen, attributing the dog with the power to see what others could or would not, that there was a 'queer, intangible something about her'.

TUNA

THE PINT-SIZE CHIWEENIE WHO'LL MELT YOUR HEART

CHIWEENIE
(CHIHUAHUA-
DACHSHUND
CROSS)

Like so many of us, Tuna, the pint-sized chiweenie, has had to go on a journey of self-acceptance. He has an exaggerated overbite, a recessed jaw, and a wrinkly neck. He isn't, in any sense of the word, a conventional beauty. But by making his oddities a virtue, he found self-love and unlikely internet notoriety. As his owner, Courtney Dasher, puts it: he's the underdog with the overbite.

Things weren't always so good for the Chihuahua-dachshund cross. He was found abandoned by the roadside in San Diego and would wriggle and crawl on his belly with worry (his temporary animal rescue nickname was Wormy). Enter Dasher, who happily agreed to foster the dog *temporarily* – but reader, she fell in love with him, and a week later, she agreed to keep him. He first appeared on Instagram in 2012 and soon did the rounds on Reddit, starring in a meme which cemented Tuna's celebrity. And boy does he look cute. He was pictured in all sorts of costumes and clever vignettes, and Tuna soon collaborated with brands and magazines, travelling the world on a press tour (it helps that chiweenies are very adaptable). Otherwise, Tuna is just like many of us: he hates mornings, loves glamping, and has a best friend called Colin.

He issues an annual calendar, is a plush toy, and, for a cool $50, he'll even record you a short personal video. With Courtney, he helps animal welfare charities like PAWS Chicago and raises awareness of the plight of rescue dogs. Two million of us follow his antics on Instagram, falling in love with his lust for life. It's enough to melt your heart.

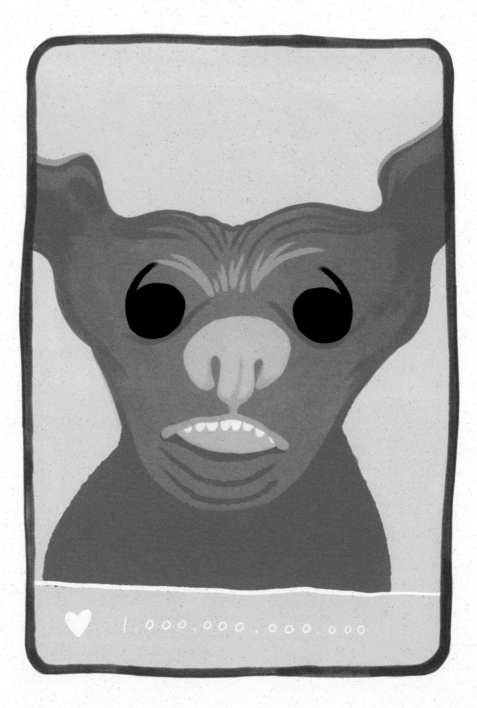

SWANSEA JACK

TO THE RESCUE WITH THE WELSH HERO

BLACK RETRIEVER

Now to Swansea Jack of Wales, the dock-dwelling shaggy-looking black retriever and one of the nation's most beloved heroes. In the 1930s Jack reportedly rescued a staggering 27 people from drowning. But how did Jack come to be a true Welsh hero again and again?

Jack lived with his owner, William Thomas, in Swansea's North Dock. The area was impoverished in this era, and many (if not most) locals did not know how to swim. Tragically, drownings were not uncommon in the river-mouth city, and cries from the waterfront were of particular interest to Jack. He was known to dive into the water and drag whoever was in difficulty to safety.

Jack's first owner was Taulford Davies, but the dog proved a little unpopular, chomping down on ducks in the local park. Jack soon moved in with William Thomas and, once a docksider, soon learnt how to swim. Jack would splash about with a group of local lads and got into the habit of holding onto their collars and dragging them to shore.

His first life saved was a 12-year-old boy, but the story wasn't widely reported. His second rescue was witnessed by a small crowd. A story soon appeared in the *Evening Post* newspaper, and Jack received an award. But it didn't stop there, and Jack saved another 25 people over the years. The awards started to pile up, including the Bravest Dog of the Year award in 1936. His memory lives on with a local memorial and Jack's indelible mark on Swansea mythology. In fact, Jack is an erstwhile name for Swansea dwellers, and fans of Swansea City Association Football Club are known as the 'Jack Army'. He remains a true Welsh hero: *Iechyd da*, Jack!

BIG BOY BAMSE

THE LIFE-SAVING, SEA-FARING WAR HERO

ST BERNARD

Bamse was a captain's dog and lived his early life on Norwegian whaling vessel *Thorodd*. The captain's daughter, Vigdis Hafto, recalled Bamse's friendly and gentle disposition, how he would happily plod and play on deck. But when WWII broke out, and *Thorodd* was requisitioned by the Royal Norwegian Navy, Bamse found a new calling. Throughout the next few years, the very big boy became a bona fide war hero.

The young St Bernard, a working dog bred in the Alps, racked up several heroic acts, from calming fighting crew members (by placing his massive paws on their shoulders) to saving another crew member from an onshore knife attack by knocking the assailant into the water. He even saved another crew member from drowning. HNoMS *Thorodd* was retrofitted as a minesweeper in Scotland and, while stationed there, Bamse would round-up the crew, apparently travelling on local buses (he even had his own bus pass) to do it. Travelling from the base to Dundee, Bamse would appear at the Bodega Bar (the Norwegian crew's favourite drinking spot) and travel back if he couldn't find them. As the ship's mascot, Bamse's legendary acts inspired the forces, and he soon became the official mascot for the whole Free Norwegian Forces during WWII.

Like many big dogs, Bamse died rather young, aged six or seven, and was buried in Montrose with full military honours and with hundreds in attendance. Since then Bamse has achieved all manner of posthumous awards, from the Norwegian Order of Dogs in 1984 and the PDSA Gold Award (the only WWII animal to have received it) to a forest in Cumbria (known as Bamse's Woods). In 2006 a life-sized bronze statue was unveiled on Montrose's Wharf Street, with the dog looking out to sea donned with the sailor's hat he was known for wearing. The ceremony had a very special guest: Vigdis Hafto, a fitting witness to her childhood dog's everlasting award.

BUDDY

THE WORLD'S FIRST SEEING-EYE DOG

In 1927, Nashville teenager Morris Frank (1908–1980) came across a newspaper article that changed his life and the lives of hundreds of others living with vision loss. The story detailed the work of Dorothy Harrison Eustis (1886–1946), an American woman training German shepherd police dogs in Switzerland, and her new trial that employed dogs as guides for blind veterans of World War I. Since he lost his vision at the age of 16, Frank had often wondered if a dog might be trained to help him further his independence, and he felt compelled to write to Eustis, the article's author.

She agreed to help, and Frank soon travelled to Switzerland to meet Eustis at her training school, Fortunate Fields. Frank returned to the USA months later with Buddy, a sprightly female German shepherd, to perform something of a press stunt in New York. Buddy led his owner across busy West Street and Broadway to the awe of a watching

crowd. He sent Eustis a telegram with just one word: 'Success'.

A big boned and imposing breed, German shepherds are incredibly intelligent, confident and near-fearless, with just enough aloofness to focus on their owner and ignore distractions. They are perfect guide dogs, and Frank and Eustis were keen to roll out their idea to help those with vision loss across America. Their school, The Seeing Eye, was founded in 1929 and became the first guide-dog school in the US.

There is something truly fruitful in the act of collaboration: if Frank had not reached out to Eustis, there might have never been a Seeing Eye school, and if Buddy hadn't worked so doggedly to keep Frank safe, the idea of the Seeing Eye dog might not have gained such support. Frank, Eustis and Buddy continued to build a Seeing Eye empire, advocating for the acceptance of guide dogs on trains and in hotels across the States – and by doing so, they changed the lives of men, women and dogs forever.

THE LITTLE BROWN DOG

THE NAMELESS STRAY WHO BECAME A FEMINIST FIREBRAND

In many ways it was a typical lecture. In 1903, in the wood-panelled teaching rooms of University College London, medical students were invited to witness a series of surgical techniques. The faint-hearted should look away now: they were performed on a live dog in a deathly process known as vivisection. Many medical colleges used vivisection as a teaching tool, but it was growing more and more unfashionable. That day, a small brown terrier lost his life, but something about that particular little stray changed the course of history.

Attending were two Swedish students, Leisa Shartau and Louise Lind-af-Hageby, from the London School of Medicine for Women. They were both dedicated anti-vivisectionists who wrote up their findings and passed their notes to Stephen Coleridge, the president of the National Anti-Vivisection Society. Coleridge was horrified. The 1876 Cruelty to Animals Act stated that the use of an animal in more than one experiment was unlawful, but it was clear that the dog had previously been under the knife. What's more, Shartau and Lind-af-Hageby observed that the dog had moved during the procedure, so Coleridge was worried the surgeon, Dr William Bayliss, had not properly anaesthetised the little terrier.

TERRIER

Coleridge spoke out publicly, only for Bayliss to sue him for libel – and win.

But it was too late: the story had reached the masses and the anti-vivisectionist movement gained huge public and celeb support (even Queen Victoria was opposed). In 1906 a statue to commemorate the little brown dog was erected in Battersea, South London, but it did little to calm the city's dog lovers and only inflamed tensions between warring political groups. Pro-vivisectionists took to the streets and soon the statue became the focus of a series of protests, riots and general naughtiness; a hotchpotch of angry, beered-up student activists, suffragettes and radicals.

At its heart, the tension was between students who saw themselves as pro-science progressives and the anti-vivisectionists themselves, and it is easy to underestimate the strength of feeling among the protesters. By December 1907 things had reached fever pitch; eye-witness Edward K Ford published a pamphlet about what unfolded. A faction of University College London students, who had come to hate the monument, went at it with a sledgehammer, each receiving a £5 fine for their trouble from the magistrate. They responded by burning the lawmaker's effigy on college grounds before marching on through the city. Over the following nights, groups of veterinary students were arrested for causing a stink, and more than 100 are said to have stormed a women's suffrage meeting in Paddington (anti-vivisectionists were often presumed to be women), with feminist foremother Millicent Fawcett attempting to calm them down.

But the little brown terrier had friends in Battersea, Ford reported,

where 'the very boys in the street take up cudgels for the dogs', and the anti-vivisectionists were undeterred. The National Anti-Vivisection Society held a ticketed meeting, only for the students to force their way in, and when Lind af-Hageby stood to speak, they let off firecrackers and stink-bombs and stood on their chairs to 'howl her down'.

The cost of policing the unrest saw the anti-vivisection issue discussed in Parliament, but the government held fast, and in 1910 the statue was quickly removed under cover of night, despite a 20,000-strong petition in favour of protecting it. With medical ethics now at the forefront of animal lovers' minds, support for anti-vivisection started to have an effect. With the introduction of a series of new laws over the decades, the practice itself has ebbed slowly from student spectacle to the shadowy corners of scientific research. But the fight is far from over. Almost 3.5 million vivisections were performed on animals in the UK in 2019, although this is thought to be the lowest number of deaths by experimentation for many decades.

Welsh author Paula S Owen's novel *Little Brown Dog* (2021) is a fictional retelling of the event, and she has said, 'The whole sorry episode is an echo, a mirror, reflecting the endless injustices and evil carried out by humans on other species throughout history.' In an act of hope, and a continuation of the work of animal heroes and great feminists like Coleridge, Shartau and Lind-af-Hageby, the author hopes to replace the stolen monument, making sure the little brown dog and his story is remembered for years to come.

32

CRACKER JACK

DOLLY PARTON'S BELOVED STRAY

UNKNOWN

Dolly Parton's 13th solo studio album, *Jolene*, was released in 1974. While most attention is reserved for the titular track – now an iconic song about the rough edges of love and jealousy – and Parton's stunning 'I Will Always Love You', there is another track that deserves our attention. 'Cracker Jack' is a jaunty song with a melancholy undercurrent that tells a simple story of bygone times, exploring 'unconditional love and a different kind of friend'. Cracker Jack is an ode to a rescue dog, a foundling from Dolly's youth who 'wasn't much to look at, but he looked alright to me'.

In the 2019 Netflix series *Heartstrings*, the legendary singer-songwriter and multi-instrumentalist discusses the real-life inspirations for some of her most well-known and best-loved songs, and she confirmed once and for all that Cracker Jack was real. The song, perhaps one of Dolly's most literal interpretations, details how she found Jack in her youth and how they supported each other through her childhood before he passed away: 'he only lives in memories now'. To Dolly, a dog is truly '...man's best friend and, well, woman's, too', and there is something almost godly about our relationship with the canine – especially one rescued from an otherwise unknown fate. 'It's no coincidence that "dog" is "God" spelled backwards,' Dolly explains. Amen to that.

33

PINKA

VIRGINIA WOOLF'S CANINE MUSE

English wordsmith and leader of the modernist literary movement Virginia Woolf (1882–1941) is author of a wealth of well-known lit classics, from *Mrs Dalloway* and *To The Lighthouse* to the gender-bending, queer-edged *Orlando*. But there is another Woolf publication that is often ignored: the author's experimental, speculative fiction project *Flush*. In it, Woolf imagines the world of Elizabeth Barrett Browning's cocker spaniel and – written from the dog's point of view – explores the life of the British poet. Less fly-on-the-wall, more dog-in-a-basket.

Woolf had an affinity with dogs and grew up surrounded by them. Virginia's childhood canine companion, a shaggy little terrier imaginatively named Shag, had a taste for rats. Other dogs were later welcomed into the clan, from a pup called Jerry to a tailless sheep dog named Gurth. The latter was Virginia's favourite, even though he was officially her sister Vanessa's dog. When Vanessa married and left their childhood home with Gurth in tow, Virginia and her brother Adrian hot-footed to Battersea Lost Dogs Home – just two years after the Little Brown Dog riots – and adopted a boxer named Hans.

When Virginia married writer Leonard Woolf, the pair first enjoyed a spaniel called Tinker (who ran away) then Grizzle, a terrier who would trot alongside Woolf on her constitutionals on the Sussex Downs. But it was Pinka, a purebred black cocker spaniel (and a gift from her sometime-lover and great friend, Vita Sackville-West), who truly stole Woolf's heart. The women famously explored their love through hundreds of poetic, meandering and heart-achingly sexy missives to each other, and Pinka – born to Pippin, Vita's own beloved dog – was a living love-letter to her beloved 'Ginia. Their relationship was something of an open secret in the bohemian social circles in which Virginia and Vita moved – and inspired the aforementioned *Orlando* – but it was through their dogs that the women found a deep kinship. Pinka and Pippin were the two women's love made real.

COCKER SPANIEL

JOFI

SIGMUND FREUD'S CANINE THERAPIST

CHOW CHOW

Lean back, take a deep breath, and tell Jofi, a chubby little chow chow, what truly ails your mind ...

In the late 1880s young neurologist and psychotherapy founder Dr Sigmund Freud made a name for himself in Vienna. Clients would visit Freud's consulting room, lie down on his couch and, using free association, bare all to the moustachioed doctor. But it was to London where Freud fled following the Nazi occupation of Austria, and there his technique became more canine-dependent.

Freud's daughter Anna had a handsome German shepherd called Wolf and her father, then in his 70s, was besotted. 'I always assert that he transferred his whole interest in me on to Wolf,' Anna wrote in 1925. But it was his own beloved dog, Jofi, a slightly overweight chow chow, who stole Freud's heart. For the seven years they were together, the pair were inseparable. 'I miss her now almost as much as my cigar,' he wrote. 'She is a charming creature, so interesting in her feminine characteristics, too, wild, impulsive, intelligent and yet not so dependent as dogs often are.'

Freud believed dogs had a calming effect on people (recent experiments indeed seem to show this could be true) and noted that they seemed to be able to read a person's emotional state. Accompanying Freud in his therapy sessions, Jofi would lie near a patient who was calm but trot off if they were anxious or distressed, and he would stretch and yawn as a session came to an end, keeping Freud's schedule running smoothly. When Jofi passed away in 1937, Freud wrote to friend and German novelist Arnold Zweig, 'Apart from any mourning, it is very unreal, and one wonders when one will get used to it.'

LITTLE MISS LOUBOUTINA

THE DOG WITH ALL THE HUGS

Although New York City is the setting for endless romcoms, it might be the last place in the world you would expect a free hug. In fact, most New Yorkers simply do not have time for things like making eye-contact, smiling, or proclaiming anything other than, 'Seriously? Get the f— outta my way!' Enter Louboutina, the shimmering, smiling golden retriever and unstoppable love-machine who set out to change all that, one hug at a time.

When Louboutina – aka Loubie – met her human, Peruvian language interpreter César Fernández-Chavéz, it was love at first sight. One year post-breakup, César was in a sad place. A friend suggested he get a puppy and, on meeting three-month-old Loubie, they fell in love in a New York minute. Dogs often initiate physical contact with their human, particularly if they feel anxious – perhaps a paw on a foot or a rump pressed lightly against your leg. Loubie, who explored the upscale sidewalks of Chelsea and Gramercy, soon started to ask César to hold her paw. And, perhaps because of the positive reaction from onlookers (who found it unbearably adorable), in 2015 Loubie's paw-hold soon turned into a hug. She fast became a local hero and an Instagram celebrity, and she now regularly poses for selfies on the streets of her local neighbourhood, with tourists – and even hard-hearted New Yorkers – stopping for a hug. The pair have been through everything together, even narrowly escaping a building fire, and their bond is undeniably strong. 'She's such a New York City diva,' says César, proudly. 'She knows daddy will do anything for her.'

BASKET

AND THE DOGS OF STEIN AND TOKLAS

American writer, novelist and playwright (and the wearer of the most severe haircut the world has ever known) Gertrude Stein (1874–1946) ruled over Paris' literary community. With her partner, Alice B Toklas, she would hold court in their apartment, delivering her scorching criticism of intellectual thought in mid-century Europe and entertaining the finest artists and writers of their day, from Pablo Picasso to Ernest Hemingway, F Scott Fitzgerald to Henri Matisse. An off-colour remark from Stein could make or break a nervous artist's reputation. But there was one major element of Stein and Toklas' life together that was beyond reproach: the two women's love of dogs.

Inside their apartment – an apartment filled with gourmet food, excellent wine, artists and writers – scampered a menagerie of dogs. There was Polpe, who loved flowers; Byron and Pepe, the sex-obsessed Chihuahuas; and head of the pack was Stein's beloved Basket, a stately standard poodle (succeeded later by Basket II). The original Basket was bought at a dog show in Paris with the intention of being trained by Toklas to carry a basket of flowers in his mouth (a feat never achieved). Stein would order Basket to be bathed every day and visiting aesthetes would be roped into their share of dog tasks – composer Paul Bowles recalled he was made to chase a post-bath Basket around the garden until he was dry (with Stein calling out encouragement from the window). Basket even starred in portrait shoots by photographic greats Cecil Beaton and Man Ray. When he died in 1937, Stein and Toklas hurriedly acquired Basket II.

Stein and Toklas, both brilliantly non-conforming, lived their lives in exactly the way they wanted. They did it with such confidence that no one in 1930s Paris raised an eyebrow at the two lesbian dog fanciers – and, in fact, their dogs seem to have inspired Stein's work. Toklas wrote: 'Basket, a large, unwieldy white poodle, still will get up on Gertrude's lap and stay there. She says that listening to the rhythm of his water-drinking made her recognise the difference between sentences and paragraphs, that paragraphs are emotional, and sentences are not.'

POODLE

RIN TIN TIN

THE IMMORTAL DOG SUPERSTAR

Hollywood film star, war survivor, and – just like the Statue of Liberty – unapologetically French, Rin Tin Tin has earned himself an enduring place in American pop culture. The handsome German shepherd was discovered on the battlefields of France during WWI and later found himself immortalised in film and literature; a brave loner; a hero outsider who had to carve his own place in the world, synonymous with the American sense of self.

US Corporal Lee Duncan rescued a poorly German shepherd and her litter of puppies from a small French village recovering from aerial bombing. He nursed them to health and, in 1919, snuck two of them – Rin Tin Tin and Nanette – aboard a ship bound for the US. Sadly, Nanette died, but Duncan was gifted another female German shepherd (Nanette II) and the odd family moved on to Los Angeles.

Duncan was convinced of Rin Tin Tin's star potential, and soon his star was in ascendance. His first film was *The Man From Hell's River* (1922), where he convincingly played a wolf, but his big break was in the smash hit *Where the North Begins* (1923). Many films followed, plus lucrative sponsorship deals. Rin Tin Tin's death in 1932 was 'we interrupt this transmission' newsflash worthy, but Tin lived on and on, embodied in the great dog's descendants and powered by Duncan, whose struggle to keep Tin's celebrity status alive is detailed in author and journalist Susan Orlean's delightful book *Rin Tin Tin: The Life, The Legend* (2012). As Orlean reports, 'he believed the dog was immortal.'

GERMAN SHEPHERD

FIDO

ITALY'S MOST LOYAL LITTLE MUTT

MUTT

Picture this: Borgo San Lorenzo, Florence, 1941. Carlo Soriani, a brick-kiln worker with a big heart, is on his way home after a hard day at work. He hears the unmistakable yelp of a dog and discovers an injured puppy with white fur and black patches by the side of the road. He takes the puppy home, and with his wife, nurses him to health. The pair become inseparable, and Carlo calls his new best friend Fido.

Carlo and Fido had a routine. They would travel to the bus stop every morning, and while Carlo went off to work at a nearby factory, Fido would mooch about the village until his best friend returned in the evening. Borgo San Lorenzo was a small village and the Sorianis and Fido were well known. In 1943 Carlo left for work as usual, but Allied forces bombed the factory, and he was killed in the blast. That evening, the small dog waited at the bus stop, looking out for his best friend.

Fido – meaning 'faithful', from Latin *fidus* – is an archetypal dog name and, although it may have fallen somewhat out of fashion in recent times, historically it was the go-to for Italian canine-lovers. In fact, if you hitched up your toga and wandered the streets of ancient Rome, you would have no doubt met a Fido or three sniffing about beneath your sandals. And it turned out to be a particularly prescient name for the Fido of this story. Carlo's dog waited and waited, returning every evening to search for him. He did this for 14 years. When Fido passed away in 1958, he was a household name in Italy, and his passing was front-page news. *Vale Fido*, one of the world's most faithful little dogs.

FOX, BALTO & TOGO

A RACE TO STOP A PANDEMIC

SIBERIAN
HUSKY

Siberian huskies are the lightest and fastest of all working dogs, with thick, frosted double-coats, almond-shaped eyes and a curious avoidance of barking in favour of letting out a lonely, urgent howl. And yet, despite their strength and wolf-like form, they are calm, non-aggressive and affectionate. They can travel near-endless distances, bolting across icefields at breakneck speed; they are unstoppable.

In 1908 Gunnar Kaasen (1882–1960), a handsome Norwegian, arrived in the USA, lured there in the gold rush. He set up in the Alaskan port town of Nome, landlocked from late autumn to late spring when the sea froze over, and Kaasen excelled in the art of mushing – the practice of using dogs to pull sleds through the snow and ice. Settlers like Kaasen and the Americans before him shared Nome with the Inupiat, the indigenous people of the region, and in 1925 a diphtheria outbreak rocked the town and both communities. Without a serum

to protect them, Nome and its inhabitants – particularly the Inupiat children – were in peril. Train and road routes were blocked and didn't reach as far north as Nome anyway and planes were grounded due to bad weather. The Alaskan governor dispatched a metal cylinder packed with 300,000 doses of serum via train from Anchorage to Nenana, a northern town as close as to Nome as possible. But Kaasen's hometown was more than 670 miles further along the Iditarod Trail, through freezing water and deathly blizzards.

Meeting the train at Nenana was dog-racing legend Leonhard Seppala, whose team of Siberian huskies was led by his beloved Togo. After Seppala and his pack set off into the snow and ice, the story hit the press. National radio stations and newspapers were wracked with the fear the musher and the serum would not reach Nome, whose inhabitants had started to succumb to the illness. Unbeknown to Seppala, who had planned to make the whole journey himself, a relay of 20 other mushers and 150 dogs had started to form along the route, and Kaasen took his place on the penultimate leg of the journey.

In Kaasen's team of 13 Siberian huskies were two particularly excellent dogs, Fox and Balto. When the relay reached Kaasen at Bluff, the musher and his pack set off, travelling through the night to reach the final relay point. The going was hard: many of the other mushers endured frostbite, frozen waters cracked open, and several of the dogs had died en route. For Kaasen, a blizzard obscured the dogs in front of him, and on one occasion the sled tipped over and he almost lost the cylinder. Kaasen reached the relay point ahead of time and, on finding the next musher sleeping, he continued for the final 25 miles with Fox and Balto leading the pack tirelessly across the frozen tundra. Ahead of schedule, the serum was delivered and Nome was saved!

The mushers and their dogs became national heroes, but it was handsome Kaasen who achieved true celebrity. However, over the next few years statues of Balto appeared across the States (resulting in some disgruntled historians who would rather the spotlight fall on Fox and Togo). The heroism of all the mushers and their dogs has never been in question. Those 150 Siberian huskies saved the lives of hundreds of Alaskans; they were simply unstoppable.

BIG BARRY

THE MOUNTAIN-RESCUE HERO

ST BERNARD

Big Barry is the Swiss action hero who saved more human lives than any other dog in history. Between 1800 and 1814, the sprightly St Bernard is thought to have rescued 40 unfortunate souls lost in the treacherous, frosted crags of the Alps, including a boy lost in a cavern of ice who rode to safety on Barry's back ... or so the legend goes.

Barry was the top graduate of the 1,000-year-old Great St Bernard Hospice, a near-magical ancient monastery teetering on the treacherous Great St Bernard Pass which connects Martigny, Switzerland to Aosta in Italy. The hospice, and its fleet of heroic dogs, is famous for breeding the St Bernard dog and providing food and shelter for passing travellers for more than 1,000 years. Some estimate that the hospice and its dogs have saved more than 2,000 lives.

In the early days the pass was a lawless place, peppered with scoundrels. But there were more dangers in this Wild West of the Alps than just being robbed: the weather was unpredictable and, in winter, blizzards could be deathly. It was for this reason the saintly figure himself, tenth-century monk Bernard de Menthon, set up a shelter on the pass to aid pilgrims on their way to Rome. Not content with building a monastery, Bernard also fought and trapped the devil (whose annoyance at that can be witnessed in the area's hellish snowstorms).

Hundreds of years later, Bernard's monks started to breed their own special mountain rescue dogs using the local large-breed cowherds, tough cart-pulling mastiffs, mongrels and such until they had perfected the St Bernard. The dogs became famous for their Alpine skills and even helped

Napoleon's troops cross the ranges, with the hospice offering full bed and breakfast (no en suite). The dogs led each group of soldiers or travellers, their weight packing down the snow and forming a path, and their incredible sense of smell helped them sniff out any potential human scallywag waiting in ambush.

The St Bernards used the same skills to hunt out the lost and near-frozen, and Barry – smaller, lighter, and more agile than the others – had the highest success rate. The number of souls he saved might be a wishful remembering, but historians agree on around 40 lost people miraculously found. And although St Bernards are often depicted with a flask of brandy around their necks, Barry was probably dispatched with a saddle pack containing bread and water.

Like all the heroic fables before him, Barry's death story is more fiction than fact. For years a tragic story abounded of an unconscious soldier licked awake by Barry's healing tongue, who woke with a start and, mistaking Baz for a wolf, plunged a knife into his heart. However, that seems to be an urban – or alpine – myth, and the true story is much kinder. Barry retired to Bern, a hundred miles from the hospice, and in 1814, plump and frosted with grey fur, he passed away peacefully.

By the 1820s Barry's line had near dwindled, and the current St Bernard, thought to be a cross with Barry's line and a Newfoundland, is a lovable version of the original, but without the strength and stamina. The hospice no longer breeds St Bernards, but nearby the Barry Foundation keeps the memory of the heroic dog alive through the rearing of a number of St Bernard dogs, some used for therapy or meet-and-greets with visitors at the museum in Martigny, and others enjoying summer holidays cavorting around the hospice. Every year they make the journey along the Great St Bernard Pass and up to the old cloisters, just like Barry would have done all those years ago.

OLD YELLER

THE HEARTBREAKING TRUE STORY

LABRADOR-MASTIFF
CROSS

If the love of a dog is so powerful, does it really matter if he ever truly existed at all? Such is the conundrum surrounding Old Yeller, the world's most-adored fictional dog. He is the heart-breaking creation of author and ex-rancher Fred Gipson, whose coming-of-age novel *Old Yeller* (1956) charts the fortunes and misfortunes of a 'dingy yellow' stray dog in rural post-Civil War USA and his relationship to his young human, Travis. But most know Yeller through the 1957 Disney movie adaptation, also written by Gipson, in which the titular dog is played by a Labrador-Mastiff cross. Both the novel and movie follow Yeller's introduction into the begrudging Coates family, his heroic antics, and the same heart-wrenching death

scene that has haunted its audience for decades.

Is *Old Yeller* a true story? Gipson's novel is clearly a work of fiction but, growing up, the author had his own bond with a dog known as Rattler, a Border collie who is thought to, in part, have inspired the writer. Works of art that centre on the relationship between a child and their dog are inevitably tinged with sadness: in these stories, kids and animals have a unique and powerful bond, something adults find hard to understand. The death of a pet is affirmed as a rite of passage, and the dog is not just a proxy for how we might feel if a human died but has its own special poignancy. Real or not, *Old Yeller* is about loss, love, and grief; no wonder it is a story that endures.

SNUPPY

THE CLONE WITH A BONE

With those long legs, lustrous tresses, and bashful, full-lashed eyes, the Afghan hound is the supermodel of the dog world, and Snuppy was no exception. Born in Seoul in 2005, Snuppy was a perfect example of his breed. Jet-black fur and artistically shaped russet-coloured eyebrows made sure he was a cut above the rest, almost as if he had been designed by a maverick scientist – and in a way he had. Snuppy was a clone.

Seoul National University (SNU) is at the forefront of gene research, and controversial professor Woo Suk Hwang oversaw Snuppy's development. Years of experiments and millions of dollars were behind his creation through somatic cell nuclear transfer. Hwang and his team harvested DNA from another dog and inserted it into a dog egg (from which the original DNA had been removed), and from this one egg, multiple cloned embryos formed. More than 1,000 were implanted in 123 female dogs but, after just a handful of pregnancies, only one puppy survived.

Nevertheless, it was a huge feat, and at an outside press conference, the newborn Snuppy (a portmanteau of SNU and puppy) cavorted across the grass, the breeze catching his gorgeous Afghan hair, before being held aloft by Hwang to the gasps of journalists. The young

dog became an instant science magazine cover star.

Of course, Snuppy wasn't the first clone. Before him scampered mice and rabbits, as well as pigs, a cow, and a sheep named Dolly. But what are the principles of cloning a dog, and what of the many failed attempts beforehand? Hwang's research straddled the controversial divide between medical ethics and animal rights, where huge forward bounds can be made for medicine but often at the expense of our canine and other animal friends. In fact, following Hwang's death in 2015, his team cloned other Afghans from Snuppy – clones of a clone, if you will – and another cloned dog, a beagle called Tegan, worryingly glowed in the dark.

Snuppy may have been the first dog clone, but he was certainly not the last. Technology is now available for pet owners to recreate their own beloved dogs, albeit for an eye-watering cost – Barbara Streisand recently chose to clone her beloved dog, Samantha. And with our love for dogs never waning, it seems we'll do anything to keep our favourite dogs in our lives forever – glow in the dark or otherwise.

PEPS

BRAVO TO WAGNER'S CANINE CO-COMPOSER

Legendary composer Richard Wagner (1813–1883) was a titan of the romantic period, creating an influential body of work that resounds to this day. He is the writer of classical music's most trippy, multi-layered, and painfully dramatic works, such as *Flight of the Valkyries* (perhaps best known in modern times as the score blasted out from the helicopter in a scene in Francis Ford Coppola's Vietnam war epic *Apocalypse Now*).

A series of rather unfortunate events shaped Wagner's talent. However, for many years Wagner's mother and siblings lived with actor and playwright Ludwig Geyer, who perhaps inspired the young man's love of music. Wagner was also a Beethoven super-fan, greatly inspired by the fellow German's work. And when he saw Wilhelmine Schröder-Devrient perform, the soprano ignited an 'angelic fire' in the young man, according to his autobiography.

But the most influential force in Wagner's life was arguably his love of dogs. Wagner and his partner, Minna Planer, had a Newfoundland – that hulking, delightfully soppy breed – named Robber, but it was his cavalier King Charles spaniel, Peps, who stole the show.

Wagner noticed Peps seemed to have an appreciation of music, reacting to different musical keys and even howling when a new piece did not suit him. Wagner, it is said, was sensitive to Peps' opinion and allowed it to inspire his work. The composer would bring household gifts when he returned from a trip and would never miss out on treating Peps as well. The pair became so attached that, when Peps fell ill, Wagner stayed by his side, putting off writing new works to spend time together instead. When Peps finally passed away, Wagner was heartbroken. He wrote to his friend that Peps 'died in my arms' and that he '... cried much, and since then I have felt bitter pain and sorrow for the dear friend of the past thirteen years'. Whatever the little dog's true influence on the work of the great composer, one thing is sure: Peps certainly put the wag in Wagner.

CAVALIER KING
CHARLES SPANIEL

OWNEY

THE MAIL-MAN-OBSESSED, WORLD-TROTTING TERRIER

TERRIER-CROSS

Mail deliverers are said to be the mortal enemies of dogs. There are stories of doorstep scuffles, unfortunate injuries and the mail itself viciously destroyed on the doormat. There might be a reason behind this feud: a mail deliverer, by the nature of their job, must approach a home then quickly leave again, and a dog barking at this perceived threat might think they have scared off an enemy. So, that dog has a tried-and-tested method for protecting their home.

But it wasn't always thus. In fact, the US Railway Mail Service has an unofficial mascot in the late, great Owney, a small and scrappy terrier-cross. In 1888 little Owney was a regular visitor to the post office in Albany, New York. His owner may well have been a post office worker, but Owney began to build relationships with the other mail clerks and soon developed an obsession with mail bags with their myriad of scents and smells.

He began to follow the bags onto mail wagons, and then – somewhat confoundingly – onto mail trains. From then on Owney began to ride with the Railway Mail Service, travelling across the States.

The story of the little dog swept through the RMS and, on meeting Owney, postal workers would attach metal tags and medals onto his collar to mark his visit. Soon Owney's fame had spread further afield, and in 1895 the postmaster of Tacoma, Washington, sent him on a round-the-world trip to promote the new Universal Postal Union. Owney travelled with his beloved mailbags on trains and steamships to Europe, the Middle East and all the way to Asia before returning more than 100 days later. After his death in 1987, his body was donated to the Smithsonian in 1911 and is now on display at the National Post Office Museum, and in 2011 Owney even appeared on a US postal stamp. A fitting tribute to the mail-loving dog.

DIAMOND

SIR ISAAC NEWTON'S DOG:
A TRUE MAVERICK

POMERANIAN

Legendary physicist Sir Isaac Newton had many obsessions: mathematics, astronomy, telescopes, the theory of gravity, falling apples ... and his greatest love, a dog named Diamond. But in 2020, with the auction of three pages of Newton's rarest writings dating back to the 1680s, a story re-emerged that suggests his relationship with Diamond may have been tested in the fieriest way. The papers – intriguingly focused on Newton's fascinations with ancient Egypt, secret codes hidden in the Pyramids' measurements and the timing of the apocalypse – are badly scorched. The culprit? Little Diamond – or so the story goes.

In J B Biot's *Life of Sir Isaac Newton* (1833), the writer notes Newton had returned home from chapel one morning to find Diamond had knocked over a candle, setting fire to Newton's papers. Two decades of hand-scribbled notes and experimentations were fire-damaged, some completely beyond repair. According to Biot, Newton is said to have exclaimed 'Oh, Diamond! Diamond! Thou little knowest the mischief thou hast done!' and took many months to emotionally recover from the loss. Luckily, Newton was undeterred in his studies and set about piecing together the wreckage. In 1687 he published his most important work, *Mathematical Principles of Natural Philosophy*, which marked out his three laws of motion, a groundbreaking theory bettered only by Einstein. The fact that none of Newton's laws are dog-related might suggest he had not fully recovered from Diamond's faux pas.

PECAS

THE DRUG LORD TURNED SUPER-SNITCH

BEAGLE CROSS

On to Colombia and the cutest drug-lord-turned-informer you'll ever have the pleasure to play fetch with. In 2014, Bogota specialist anti-narcotics police were on the hunt for a notorious nine-man drug-trafficking gang. Following a successful operation, several arrests, and a huge haul of drugs, they found themselves in the possession of something unexpected. Enter the excitable and heart-meltingly friendly beagle cross with long floppy ears and a spotted Dalmatian-like coat known as 'Pecas', or Freckles in English. He had been trained to protect his owner, the alleged trafficker, by warning him

about suspicious activities and keeping him one step ahead of the law.

With no home and his original owner now indisposed, Pecas was at a loose end, but the Bogota police had a brilliant idea. They enrolled Pecas at Police Academy, introducing him to other cadet dogs in the lush, green facility outside of the city. He loved his new home, and his handlers were able to retrain him to do something quite heroic, using his incredible sense of smell on search and rescue missions. Old dog, new tricks.

CHECKERS

NIXON'S FIRST POLITICAL SCANDAL

COCKER SPANIEL

Before Watergate, the scandal that saw the shock resignation of President Richard Nixon, the politician weathered another sticky situation. In the early days of his career, accusations of dodgy dealings threatened to derail Nixon's vice-presidential bid, seeing him take to the airwaves for a national address to clear his name. But what was at the at the heart of the alleged political misconduct? A little cocker spaniel called Checkers.

During his first election campaign, Nixon, then a California senator, promised to stamp out political corruption – 'drain the swamp', if you will. But Nixon had his own wealthy backers, and a fund had been put together which came under great scrutiny from his opponents. The fund was not illegal, but Nixon's spending habits seemed a little dubious. In September 1952 the press got hold of the story and Nixon's popularity was under grave threat. With weeks to go until the election, he raised a further $75,000 to secure a 30-minute slot on TV and radio to tell his side of the story. More than 60 million Americans tuned in and his ingenious speech – deft, knowing and emotional – secured him the vice-presidency.

Laying his finances bare, Nixon described a surprisingly humble situation, dispelling the idea that politicians all have wealthy backgrounds. But there was one thing he refused to 'return'. Looking straight down the camera, Nixon said, 'We did get something – a gift – after the election. A man down in Texas heard Pat [Nixon's wife] on the radio mention the fact that our two youngsters would like to have a dog.' He went on to describe how a little terrier had been sent to Nixon's home in Baltimore, 'and our little girl – Tricia, the six-year-old – named it Checkers. And you know, the kids, like all kids, love the dog and I just want to say this right now, that regardless of what they say about it, we're gonna keep it.' And with one canine anecdote, Nixon tugged at the heartstrings of Americans until they snapped. Although Checkers was never actually under threat, Nixon's popularity was restored, and he swept to victory that November.

Checkers passed away in 1964, four years before Nixon became president, and never got to pee on the White House lawn with the Nixon family's Irish setter, little Yorkie, and poodle. His legacy, however, is great – not just through Nixon's emotional outpouring (similar political manoeuvres are now known as a 'Checkers speech') but how he resonated with the American public. Sometimes, we might just risk everything for our dogs.

BOBBY

THE ALMOST TRUE TALE OF GREYFRIARS BOBBY

To Edinburgh, Scotland, in the late 1850s, and the heartbreaking tale of a wee Skye terrier whose selfless act of loyalty has inspired any number of books, films and Edinburgh traditions, making him one of the world's most famous dogs.

One night in 1858, Bobby's owner John Gray, aka 'Auld Jock', a local farm labourer, took ill and soon died from tuberculosis. Legend has it that soon after Gray's funeral, Bobby was found pining by his grave in Greyfriars cemetery and held vigil there for 14 long years, be the weather fair or *dreich* (fantastic Scots term for utterly miserable), breaking only for his lunchtime meal, marked by the One o'Clock Gun fired from Edinburgh Castle. He became the city's unofficial mascot and, after his death in 1872, even acquired his own tiny bronze statue on the busy George IV Bridge (a landmark more popular than its size suggests). But much like the statue's nose (which visitors still like to touch for luck), much of Bobby's story had already been buffed to a high shine by the time

an American novelist came to town in the hopes Bobby's story would go global. Eleanor Stackhouse Atkinson's *Greyfriars Bobby* (1912) was a bestseller and is now the dominant account of the little dog's remarkable life.

Others are more sceptical, pointing out inaccuracies in Atkinson's version, disputing Auld Jock's profession (he was probably a policeman) and even suggesting that there may have been several Bobbys over the years. Scottish writer Gilbert Summers points out the 'loyal dog who waits for dead owner' is a well-known 'folk-motif', and the late historian Forbes Macgregor wrote a book, *Greyfriars Bobby: The Real Story at Last* (rev. 2002), which unearthed accounts deep in the archives of locals taking turns to care for Bobby, who was known to accept the offer of a meal and a warm bed for the night. For all the shining-up Bobby's story has undergone over the years, it seems the real tale is a simple one: a little shaggy dog who loved his master long after he had departed.

STUBBY

SALUTE THE ALL-AMERICAN WAR HERO SERGEANT

BRINDLE BULL TERRIER

Let's salute Sergeant Stubby, one of the most famous soldiers in US history. Stubby's tireless heroism during WWI is the stuff of legend: he would alert his fellow combatants to mustard-gas attacks, find and calm battle-wounded soldiers, and he even caught a fleeing enemy by the seat of his pants. And he didn't let the fact that he was a mere brindle bull terrier stop him from achieving his dreams.

Stubby was the mascot of the 102nd Infantry, but he was clearly so much more than that. Discovered wandering the grounds of the Yale campus by soldiers-in-training in New Haven, Connecticut, in 1917, Stubby (for he was small and a little on the heavy side) became particularly enamoured with Corporal James Robert Conroy. The two grew to be inseparable and Conroy stowed Stubby away in a coal bin on a troop ship bound for France. Stubby snuggled into Conroy's coat as they embarked but he was soon discovered by his commanding officer. Stubby saluted him, just as Conroy had taught him at Yale; the commanding officer clearly found it too adorable to bear and thus began the dog's first military tour.

Stubby's heroism on the battle fields made headline news at home. Readers were thrilled to read his antics and despaired when he was injured by a grenade. He thankfully recovered, and when he caught a German spy (by biting his bum and refusing to let go), Stubby earned the title of sergeant. Smuggled home 18 months after his arrival, Sergeant Stubby was a national hero. Weighed down with medals, he met three sitting presidents and was twice a guest of honour at the White House. Not bad for a stubby bull terrier. He was even a lifetime member of the American Red Cross and the YMCA until his peaceful death in 1926. At ease, soldier.

BIERKA

AND THE TRUE STORY OF PAVLOV'S DOGS

VARIOUS

Many of us spend hours interpreting the behaviour of our dogs. Just what the heck are they trying to tell us? What does that disgruntled side-eye mean? That paw finding its way to our foot? And does that coquettish 'who, me?' expression mean one should search the apartment for a fresh dog-made surprise? In other words, we constantly seek out ways in which dogs can be read as human. But in the early 1900s Russian physiologist Ivan Pavlov (1849–1936) had other ideas, and – armed with a buzzer, a dog bowl, a mutt and a curious obsession with dog drool – revealed how humans are, in fact, just like dogs.

The experiment – wonderfully simple – required a buzzer, some delicious food and the odd hungry dog. Again and again Pavlov would press the buzzer just before he fed a dog and noted that the pup soon started to salivate on hearing it, knowing it was about to be treated. Pavlov proposed the dog had started to associate the sound with being fed and the beginnings of classic conditioning and associative learning were formed.

Pavlov's findings were ground-breaking, and they formed the foundation of much of contemporary psychology's theories, therapies and studies. In fact Pavlov won a Nobel Prize in 1904 for his efforts, and his work even filtered through to wider society, making him a household name. But, as so often with scientific breakthroughs that involve the brilliance of animals, few had sought to record the identity of the dogs involved.

We can thank American neurobiologist Tim Tully with rediscovering the names of Pavlov's dogs. In the early 1990s, Tully travelled to Russia to do two things: lecture at the Pavlov Institute in Koltushi and to learn the names of Pavlov's dogs to help with his own whimsical project. He wanted to name his own fruit fly-related genes (apparently drosophologists like

Tully adore marking new discoveries with interesting or meaningful names) with those of Pavlov's famous dogs – but where to start? After some initial struggles, near the end of his trip he found himself in the scientist's old apartment, then something of a museum, and with the help of a guide the full story started to take shape.

For one thing, Pavlov's dogs were many. Tully remembers being handed photographs of the pack, noting the lauded scientist had more than 40 during the time of his experiments, from Bierka (arguably the most famous) to Arleekin ('clown') and Barbus ('big dog') through to Murashka ('cute little thing'). And Pavlov's theory turned out to be something of a happy accident. Rather sniffy towards the relatively new science of psychology, Pavlov had instead set out to measure the salivary responses in dogs. But rather than noting how the dogs started to salivate when their dinner was presented to them, Pavlov saw how it would start as soon as the dogs heard the footsteps of Pavlov's assistants walking down the hall with their food. Pavlov replaced the footsteps with his buzzer and his discovery became clear.

In 1924 a less than happy accident occurred that seemed to add more colour to Pavlov's theories. During a flood, Pavlov's laboratory in Petrograd was partially submerged and many of the dogs were trapped almost underwater for hours, until they were saved. Pavlov's assistants, who the dogs knew and trusted, had to save them

by pulling them briefly underwater to safety. It would have been terrifying for the dogs and, when the laboratory was open again, Pavlov noted something startling. The dogs no longer salivated when the assistants approached, nor seemed excited. Stress had completely broken their conditioning.

In modern times, Pavlov's research still excites – not just his work into dog drool and classic conditioning, but some are re-examining his work as an example of our complex ethical relationship with animals. In the University of Brighton lecturer Matthew Adams' *The Kingdom of Dogs: Understanding Pavlov's experiments as human-animal relationships*, he walks through Pavlov's experiments with a more critical eye. Why don't we look beyond the results and examine what exactly running an experiment like Pavlov's says about us? Others, like Pavlov biographer Daniel P Todes, point out Pavlov's infamous temper tantrums, and how – with the official 'happy accident' story of his work – we like to forget how the dogs in his drool studies were treated nothing less than abysmally. Through Pavlov's work and our own everyday knowledge of living with dogs, it's clear: dogs can give us such incredible affection and near unwavering trust, they are susceptible to stress and would do almost anything for us. Perhaps, if we can read them at all, they are trying to tell us just that.

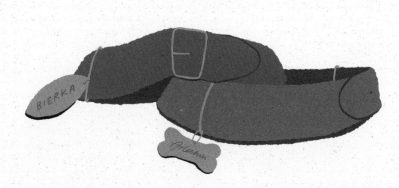

ABOUT DAN JONES

Dan Jones is a best-selling author and dog-lover. He lives in London and writes about booze, grooming, style, queer culture, Princess Diana, and why dogs are so ace.

ACKNOWLEDGEMENTS

Thank you to Louise, Sophie, Jackie and Lindsey, Pip and Jacob, Meghan, Zee, Hannah, Lottie, Gina, Issy, Toby, Cate, Kate P, my partner, Tom, and anyone else who's had the good fortune to care for my dog, Gary.

Thanks also to Welbeck's Kate Pollard and Matt Tomlinson, Art Director Evi O and her studio of dog-lovers.

And, of course, thanks to the little man himself, the goodest good boy of them all: my Border terrier, Gary.

Published in 2022 by OH Editions
Part of Welbeck Publishing Group.
Based in London and Sydney.
www.welbeckpublishing.com

Publisher: Kate Pollard
Editor: Matt Tomlinson
Designer: Evi O. Studio | Susan Le & Kait Polkinghorne
Illustrator: Evi O. Studio | Kait Polkinghorne
Production controller: Jess Brisley

Printed and bound by RR Donnelley

MIX
Paper from
responsible sources
FSC® C144853
FSC
www.fsc.org

10 9 8 7 6 5 4 3 2 1